The 3-Minute OUTER SPACE LEADERSHIP JOURNAL

FOR KIDS

✏️ This Awesome Journal Belongs To:

Blank Classic

The 3-Minute Outer Space
        Leadership Journal for Kids
116 numbered pages - 120 total pages
A5 (5.83 x 8.27)

Design © 2021 Blank Classic

Blank Classic

Mailing address:
Blank Classic
PO BOX 4608
Main Station Terminal
349 West Georgia Street
Vancouver, BC
Canada, V6B 4A1

Cover design by: Lauren Dick
Interior design by: Lauren Dick

ISBN: 978-1-77476-180-9

FIRST EDITION / FIRST PRINTING

I CAN... 
SHOW KINDNESS
SET GOALS
BE A GOOD LISTENER
INSPIRE PEOPLE
LEARN FROM OTHERS
BELIEVE IN MYSELF
SET A GOOD EXAMPLE
EMBRACE DIFFERENCES
ADMIT MISTAKES
HELP PEOPLE
BECAUSE I AM A LEADER
SIGNED,

DATE: S M T W TH F S ___ / ___ / ___

OVERALL TODAY WAS: ☆ ☆ ☆ ☆ ☆

👍 TODAY'S TRIUMPHS

👎 TODAY'S CHALLENGES

💡 WHAT I LEARNED FROM TODAY:

🏆 MY TOP GOAL FOR TOMORROW:

ASTRO CAT 2.0

OVERALL TODAY WAS: ☆ ☆ ☆ ☆ ☆

👍 **TODAY'S TRIUMPHS**

👎 **TODAY'S CHALLENGES**

💡 **WHAT I LEARNED FROM TODAY:**

🏆 **MY TOP GOAL FOR TOMORROW:**

DRAW ABOUT IT

DATE: S M T W TH F S __ / __ / __

👍 **TODAY'S TRIUMPHS**

👎 **TODAY'S CHALLENGES**

💡 WHAT I LEARNED FROM TODAY:

🏆 MY TOP GOAL FOR TOMORROW:

ASTRO CAT 2.0.

DATE: S M T W TH F S ___ / ___ / ___

OVERALL TODAY WAS: ☆ ☆ ☆ ☆ ☆

👍 TODAY'S TRIUMPHS

____
____
____
____
____
____
____
____
____

👎 TODAY'S CHALLENGES

____
____
____
____
____
____
____
____
____

💡 WHAT I LEARNED FROM TODAY:

____

🏆 MY TOP GOAL FOR TOMORROW:

____

DRAW ABOUT IT

DATE: S M T W TH F S __ / __ / __

OVERALL TODAY WAS: ☆ ☆ ☆ ☆ ☆

👍 TODAY'S TRIUMPHS

👎 TODAY'S CHALLENGES

💡 WHAT I LEARNED FROM TODAY:

🏆 MY TOP GOAL FOR TOMORROW:

DRAW ABOUT IT

DATE: S M T W TH F S __ / __ / __

OVERALL TODAY WAS: ☆ ☆ ☆ ☆ ☆

👍 TODAY'S TRIUMPHS

👎 TODAY'S CHALLENGES

💡 WHAT I LEARNED FROM TODAY:

🏆 MY TOP GOAL FOR TOMORROW:

DRAW ABOUT IT

DATE: S M T W TH F S __/__/__

OVERALL TODAY WAS:

TODAY'S TRIUMPHS

TODAY'S CHALLENGES

WHAT I LEARNED FROM TODAY:

MY TOP GOAL FOR TOMORROW:

DRAW ABOUT IT

DATE: S M T W TH F S __ / __ / __

OVERALL TODAY WAS: ☆ ☆ ☆ ☆ ☆

👍 TODAY'S TRIUMPHS

👎 TODAY'S CHALLENGES

💡 WHAT I LEARNED FROM TODAY:

🏆 MY TOP GOAL FOR TOMORROW:

DRAW ABOUT IT

DATE: S M T W TH F S __ / __ /__

OVERALL TODAY WAS: ☆ ☆ ☆ ☆ ☆

👍 TODAY'S TRIUMPHS

👎 TODAY'S CHALLENGES

💡 WHAT I LEARNED FROM TODAY:

🏆 MY TOP GOAL FOR TOMORROW:

DRAW ABOUT IT

DATE: S M T W TH F S __ / __ / __

👍 OVERALL TODAY WAS: ☆ ☆ ☆ ☆ ☆

👍 TODAY'S TRIUMPHS

👎 TODAY'S CHALLENGES

💡 WHAT I LEARNED FROM TODAY:

🏆 MY TOP GOAL FOR TOMORROW:

DRAW ABOUT IT

DATE: S M T W TH F S __ / __ / __

🏆 OVERALL TODAY WAS: ☆ ☆ ☆ ☆ ☆

👍 TODAY'S TRIUMPHS

👎 TODAY'S CHALLENGES

💡 WHAT I LEARNED FROM TODAY:

🏆 MY TOP GOAL FOR TOMORROW:

DRAW ABOUT IT

DATE: S M T W TH F S   __ / __ / __

OVERALL TODAY WAS: ☆ ☆ ☆ ☆ ☆

👍 TODAY'S TRIUMPHS

____

____

____

____

____

____

____

____

👎 TODAY'S CHALLENGES

____

____

____

____

____

____

____

____

💡 WHAT I LEARNED FROM TODAY:

____

🏆 MY TOP GOAL FOR TOMORROW:

____

DRAW ABOUT IT

DATE: S M T W TH F S __ / __ / __

🏆 OVERALL TODAY WAS: ☆ ☆ ☆ ☆ ☆

👍 TODAY'S TRIUMPHS

👎 TODAY'S CHALLENGES

💡 WHAT I LEARNED FROM TODAY:

🏆 MY TOP GOAL FOR TOMORROW:

DRAW ABOUT IT

DATE: S M T W TH F S __ / __ / __

OVERALL TODAY WAS:

TODAY'S TRIUMPHS

TODAY'S CHALLENGES

WHAT I LEARNED FROM TODAY:

MY TOP GOAL FOR TOMORROW:

DRAW ABOUT IT

OVERALL TODAY WAS: ☆ ☆ ☆ ☆ ☆

👍 TODAY'S TRIUMPHS

👎 TODAY'S CHALLENGES

💡 WHAT I LEARNED FROM TODAY:

🏆 MY TOP GOAL FOR TOMORROW:

DRAW ABOUT IT

DATE: S M T W TH F S __/__/__

OVERALL TODAY WAS: ☆ ☆ ☆ ☆ ☆

👍 TODAY'S TRIUMPHS

👎 TODAY'S CHALLENGES

💡 WHAT I LEARNED FROM TODAY:

🏆 MY TOP GOAL FOR TOMORROW:

DRAW ABOUT IT

DATE: S M T W TH F S __ / __ / __

OVERALL TODAY WAS: ☆ ☆ ☆ ☆ ☆

👍 TODAY'S TRIUMPHS

👎 TODAY'S CHALLENGES

💡 WHAT I LEARNED FROM TODAY:

🏆 MY TOP GOAL FOR TOMORROW:

DRAW ABOUT IT

OVERALL TODAY WAS: ☆ ☆ ☆ ☆ ☆

👍 TODAY'S TRIUMPHS

____
____
____
____
____
____
____
____

👎 TODAY'S CHALLENGES

____
____
____
____
____
____
____
____

💡 WHAT I LEARNED FROM TODAY:

____

🏆 MY TOP GOAL FOR TOMORROW:

____

DRAW ABOUT IT

DATE: S M T W TH F S __ / __ / __

📊 OVERALL TODAY WAS: ☆ ☆ ☆ ☆ ☆

👍 TODAY'S TRIUMPHS

👎 TODAY'S CHALLENGES

💡 WHAT I LEARNED FROM TODAY:

🏆 MY TOP GOAL FOR TOMORROW:

DRAW ABOUT IT

DATE: S M T W TH F S __ / __ / __

OVERALL TODAY WAS: ☆ ☆ ☆ ☆ ☆

TODAY'S TRIUMPHS

TODAY'S CHALLENGES

WHAT I LEARNED FROM TODAY:

MY TOP GOAL FOR TOMORROW:

DRAW ABOUT IT

🏆 OVERALL TODAY WAS: ☆ ☆ ☆ ☆ ☆

👍 TODAY'S TRIUMPHS

____

____

____

____

____

____

____

👎 TODAY'S CHALLENGES

____

____

____

____

____

____

____

💡 WHAT I LEARNED FROM TODAY:

____

🏆 MY TOP GOAL FOR TOMORROW:

____

DRAW ABOUT IT

DATE: S M T W TH F S __/__/__

🏆 OVERALL TODAY WAS: ☆ ☆ ☆ ☆ ☆

👍 TODAY'S TRIUMPHS

____
____
____
____
____
____
____
____
____

👎 TODAY'S CHALLENGES

____
____
____
____
____
____
____
____
____

💡 WHAT I LEARNED FROM TODAY:

____

🏆 MY TOP GOAL FOR TOMORROW:

____

DRAW ABOUT IT

DATE: S M T W TH F S   __ / __ / __

OVERALL TODAY WAS:

👍 TODAY'S TRIUMPHS

👎 TODAY'S CHALLENGES

💡 WHAT I LEARNED FROM TODAY:

🏆 MY TOP GOAL FOR TOMORROW:

DRAW ABOUT IT

DATE: S M T W TH F S __/__/__

🧱 OVERALL TODAY WAS: ☆ ☆ ☆ ☆ ☆

👍 TODAY'S TRIUMPHS

👎 TODAY'S CHALLENGES

💡 WHAT I LEARNED FROM TODAY:

🏆 MY TOP GOAL FOR TOMORROW:

DRAW ABOUT IT

DATE: S M T W TH F S __ / __ / __

OVERALL TODAY WAS: ☆ ☆ ☆ ☆ ☆

👍 TODAY'S TRIUMPHS

👎 TODAY'S CHALLENGES

💡 WHAT I LEARNED FROM TODAY:

🏆 MY TOP GOAL FOR TOMORROW:

DRAW ABOUT IT

DATE: S M T W TH F S __ / __ / __

OVERALL TODAY WAS: ☆ ☆ ☆ ☆ ☆

👍 TODAY'S TRIUMPHS

👎 TODAY'S CHALLENGES

💡 WHAT I LEARNED FROM TODAY:

🏆 MY TOP GOAL FOR TOMORROW:

DRAW ABOUT IT

DATE: S M T W TH F S   __ / __ / __

OVERALL TODAY WAS: ☆ ☆ ☆ ☆ ☆

👍 TODAY'S TRIUMPHS

👎 TODAY'S CHALLENGES

💡 WHAT I LEARNED FROM TODAY:

🏆 MY TOP GOAL FOR TOMORROW:

DRAW ABOUT IT

DATE: S M T W TH F S __ / __ / __

🏆 OVERALL TODAY WAS: ☆ ☆ ☆ ☆ ☆

👍 TODAY'S TRIUMPHS

____
____
____
____
____
____
____

👎 TODAY'S CHALLENGES

____
____
____
____
____
____
____

💡 WHAT I LEARNED FROM TODAY:

____

🏆 MY TOP GOAL FOR TOMORROW:

____

DRAW ABOUT IT

DATE: S M T W TH F S __ / __ / __

🏆 OVERALL TODAY WAS: ☆ ☆ ☆ ☆ ☆

👍 TODAY'S TRIUMPHS

👎 TODAY'S CHALLENGES

💡 WHAT I LEARNED FROM TODAY:

🏆 MY TOP GOAL FOR TOMORROW:

DRAW ABOUT IT

DATE: S M T W TH F S __ / __ / __

OVERALL TODAY WAS: ☆ ☆ ☆ ☆ ☆

👍 TODAY'S TRIUMPHS

👎 TODAY'S CHALLENGES

💡 WHAT I LEARNED FROM TODAY:

🏆 MY TOP GOAL FOR TOMORROW:

DRAW ABOUT IT

DATE: S M T W TH F S ___/___/___

OVERALL TODAY WAS: ☆ ☆ ☆ ☆ ☆

👍 TODAY'S TRIUMPHS

👎 TODAY'S CHALLENGES

💡 WHAT I LEARNED FROM TODAY:

🏆 MY TOP GOAL FOR TOMORROW:

DRAW ABOUT IT

DATE: S M T W TH F S __ / __ / __

🏆 OVERALL TODAY WAS: ☆ ☆ ☆ ☆ ☆

👍 TODAY'S TRIUMPHS

👎 TODAY'S CHALLENGES

💡 WHAT I LEARNED FROM TODAY:

🏆 MY TOP GOAL FOR TOMORROW:

DRAW ABOUT IT

DATE: S M T W TH F S __/__/__

👍 TODAY'S TRIUMPHS

👎 TODAY'S CHALLENGES

💡 WHAT I LEARNED FROM TODAY:

🏆 MY TOP GOAL FOR TOMORROW:

DRAW ABOUT IT

DATE: S M T W TH F S __ / __ / __

OVERALL TODAY WAS: ☆ ☆ ☆ ☆ ☆

👍 TODAY'S TRIUMPHS

👎 TODAY'S CHALLENGES

💡 WHAT I LEARNED FROM TODAY:

🏆 MY TOP GOAL FOR TOMORROW:

DRAW ABOUT IT

DATE: S M T W TH F S __/__/__

OVERALL TODAY WAS: ☆ ☆ ☆ ☆ ☆

👍 TODAY'S TRIUMPHS

____
____
____
____
____
____
____
____

👎 TODAY'S CHALLENGES

____
____
____
____
____
____
____
____

💡 WHAT I LEARNED FROM TODAY:

____

🏆 MY TOP GOAL FOR TOMORROW:

____

DRAW ABOUT IT

ASTRO CAT 2.0

DATE: S M T W TH F S __/__/__

OVERALL TODAY WAS: ☆ ☆ ☆ ☆ ☆

👍 TODAY'S TRIUMPHS

👎 TODAY'S CHALLENGES

💡 WHAT I LEARNED FROM TODAY:

🏆 MY TOP GOAL FOR TOMORROW:

DRAW ABOUT IT

DATE: S M T W TH F S __ / __ / __

OVERALL TODAY WAS: ☆ ☆ ☆ ☆ ☆

👍 TODAY'S TRIUMPHS

👎 TODAY'S CHALLENGES

💡 WHAT I LEARNED FROM TODAY:

🏆 MY TOP GOAL FOR TOMORROW:

DRAW ABOUT IT

DATE: S M T W TH F S __ / __ / __

OVERALL TODAY WAS: ☆ ☆ ☆ ☆ ☆

👍 TODAY'S TRIUMPHS

👎 TODAY'S CHALLENGES

💡 WHAT I LEARNED FROM TODAY:

🏆 MY TOP GOAL FOR TOMORROW:

DRAW ABOUT IT

DATE: S M T W TH F S __ / __ / __

🏆 OVERALL TODAY WAS: ☆ ☆ ☆ ☆ ☆

👍 TODAY'S TRIUMPHS

👎 TODAY'S CHALLENGES

💡 WHAT I LEARNED FROM TODAY:

🏆 MY TOP GOAL FOR TOMORROW:

DRAW ABOUT IT

DATE: S M T W TH F S   __ / __ / __

OVERALL TODAY WAS: ☆ ☆ ☆ ☆ ☆

👍 TODAY'S TRIUMPHS

____
____
____
____
____
____
____
____

👎 TODAY'S CHALLENGES

____
____
____
____
____
____
____
____

💡 WHAT I LEARNED FROM TODAY:

____

🏆 MY TOP GOAL FOR TOMORROW:

____

DRAW ABOUT IT

DATE: S M T W TH F S __/__/__

OVERALL TODAY WAS: ☆ ☆ ☆ ☆ ☆

👍 TODAY'S TRIUMPHS

👎 TODAY'S CHALLENGES

💡 WHAT I LEARNED FROM TODAY:

🏆 MY TOP GOAL FOR TOMORROW:

DRAW ABOUT IT

DATE: S M T W TH F S __ / __ /__

🧊 OVERALL TODAY WAS: ☆ ☆ ☆ ☆ ☆

👍 TODAY'S TRIUMPHS

👎 TODAY'S CHALLENGES

💡 WHAT I LEARNED FROM TODAY:

🏆 MY TOP GOAL FOR TOMORROW:

DRAW ABOUT IT

DATE: S M T W TH F S __ / __ /__

OVERALL TODAY WAS: ☆ ☆ ☆ ☆ ☆

👍 TODAY'S TRIUMPHS

👎 TODAY'S CHALLENGES

💡 WHAT I LEARNED FROM TODAY:

🏆 MY TOP GOAL FOR TOMORROW:

DRAW ABOUT IT

DATE: S M T W TH F S ___ / ___ / ___

🏆 OVERALL TODAY WAS: ☆ ☆ ☆ ☆ ☆

👍 TODAY'S TRIUMPHS

👎 TODAY'S CHALLENGES

💡 WHAT I LEARNED FROM TODAY:

🏆 MY TOP GOAL FOR TOMORROW:

DRAW ABOUT IT

DATE: S M T W TH F S   __ / __ / __

OVERALL TODAY WAS: ☆ ☆ ☆ ☆ ☆

TODAY'S TRIUMPHS

TODAY'S CHALLENGES

WHAT I LEARNED FROM TODAY:

MY TOP GOAL FOR TOMORROW:

DRAW ABOUT IT

OVERALL TODAY WAS: ☆ ☆ ☆ ☆ ☆

👍 TODAY'S TRIUMPHS

👎 TODAY'S CHALLENGES

💡 WHAT I LEARNED FROM TODAY:

🏆 MY TOP GOAL FOR TOMORROW:

DRAW ABOUT IT

DATE: S   M   T   W   TH   F   S   __ / __ / __

OVERALL TODAY WAS: ☆ ☆ ☆ ☆ ☆

👍 **TODAY'S TRIUMPHS**

👎 **TODAY'S CHALLENGES**

💡 **WHAT I LEARNED FROM TODAY:**

🏆 **MY TOP GOAL FOR TOMORROW:**

DRAW ABOUT IT

DATE: S M T W TH F S __ / __ / __

OVERALL TODAY WAS: ☆ ☆ ☆ ☆ ☆

👍 TODAY'S TRIUMPHS

👎 TODAY'S CHALLENGES

💡 WHAT I LEARNED FROM TODAY:

🏆 MY TOP GOAL FOR TOMORROW:

DRAW ABOUT IT

DATE: S M T W TH F S __ / __ / __

🏆 OVERALL TODAY WAS: ☆ ☆ ☆ ☆ ☆

👍 TODAY'S TRIUMPHS

👎 TODAY'S CHALLENGES

💡 WHAT I LEARNED FROM TODAY:

🏆 MY TOP GOAL FOR TOMORROW:

DRAW ABOUT IT

DATE: S M T W TH F S   __ / __ / __

🏆 OVERALL TODAY WAS: ☆ ☆ ☆ ☆ ☆

👍 TODAY'S TRIUMPHS

👎 TODAY'S CHALLENGES

💡 WHAT I LEARNED FROM TODAY:

🏆 MY TOP GOAL FOR TOMORROW:

DRAW ABOUT IT

DATE: S M T W TH F S __ / __ / __

OVERALL TODAY WAS: ☆ ☆ ☆ ☆ ☆

👍 TODAY'S TRIUMPHS

👎 TODAY'S CHALLENGES

💡 WHAT I LEARNED FROM TODAY:

🏆 MY TOP GOAL FOR TOMORROW:

DRAW ABOUT IT

DATE: S M T W TH F S __ / __ / __

OVERALL TODAY WAS: ☆ ☆ ☆ ☆ ☆

👍 TODAY'S TRIUMPHS

👎 TODAY'S CHALLENGES

💡 WHAT I LEARNED FROM TODAY:

🏆 MY TOP GOAL FOR TOMORROW:

DRAW ABOUT IT

DATE: S M T W TH F S __ / __ / __

OVERALL TODAY WAS: ☆ ☆ ☆ ☆ ☆

👍 TODAY'S TRIUMPHS

👎 TODAY'S CHALLENGES

💡 WHAT I LEARNED FROM TODAY:

🏆 MY TOP GOAL FOR TOMORROW:

DRAW ABOUT IT
ASTRO CAT 2.0.

DATE: S M T W TH F S __ / __ /__

OVERALL TODAY WAS: ☆ ☆ ☆ ☆ ☆

👍 TODAY'S TRIUMPHS

👎 TODAY'S CHALLENGES

💡 WHAT I LEARNED FROM TODAY:

🏆 MY TOP GOAL FOR TOMORROW:

DRAW ABOUT IT

OVERALL TODAY WAS: ☆ ☆ ☆ ☆ ☆

👍 TODAY'S TRIUMPHS

👎 TODAY'S CHALLENGES

💡 WHAT I LEARNED FROM TODAY:

🏆 MY TOP GOAL FOR TOMORROW:

DRAW ABOUT IT

DATE: S M T W TH F S __ / __ / __

OVERALL TODAY WAS: ☆ ☆ ☆ ☆ ☆

👍 TODAY'S TRIUMPHS

👎 TODAY'S CHALLENGES

💡 WHAT I LEARNED FROM TODAY:

🏆 MY TOP GOAL FOR TOMORROW:

DRAW ABOUT IT

DATE: S M T W TH F S __ / __ / __

OVERALL TODAY WAS: ☆ ☆ ☆ ☆ ☆

👍 TODAY'S TRIUMPHS

👎 TODAY'S CHALLENGES

💡 WHAT I LEARNED FROM TODAY:

🏆 MY TOP GOAL FOR TOMORROW:

DRAW ABOUT IT

DATE: S M T W TH F S __ / __ / __

OVERALL TODAY WAS: ☆ ☆ ☆ ☆ ☆

TODAY'S TRIUMPHS

TODAY'S CHALLENGES

WHAT I LEARNED FROM TODAY:

MY TOP GOAL FOR TOMORROW:

DRAW ABOUT IT

www.ingramcontent.com/pod-product-compliance
Lightning Source LLC
Chambersburg PA
CBHW060953050726
47592CB00003B/1209